Dear Mark,

Congratulations and
best wishes to you
as you graduate from
East Central!

Sincerely in Christ,

Rev. Earl Ferguson

DIR

**A Gif

DIRECTIONS

A Gift Book for Graduates

LeRoy Koopman

BAKER BOOK HOUSE
Grand Rapids, Michigan 49506

Scripture references, unless otherwise noted, are from the Revised Standard Version of the Bible, copyrighted 1946, 1952, ©
1971, 1973.

To my two favorite graduates,
Kendall and Lori

Contents

A Prayer at the End

For classrooms and gymnasiums,
    libraries and study halls,
    laboratories and cafeterias,
        We thank you, Lord.

For the joy of discovery,
    the excitement of knowledge,
    the satisfaction of new skills,
        We thank you, Lord.

For the insights of history,
    the wisdom of thinkers,
    the beauty of the arts,
    the wonders of the world,
        We thank you, Lord.

For teachers who cared enough to discipline,
    for administrators who smiled,
    for supervisors who listened,
    for friends who encouraged,
    for parents who loved,
        We thank you, Lord.

of the School Year

For the freedom to disagree,
    to debate,
    to doubt,
        We thank you, Lord.

That we may have the desire
    to apply what we have been taught,
    to keep on learning,
    to keep expanding our concern,
        We ask your help.

That we may learn how to live
    as well as how to make a living;
that we may learn wisdom
    as well as knowledge;
that we may be concerned about our souls
    as well as about our minds and bodies;
        We ask your grace.

A Formula
for Facing the Future

You have your suitcases packed, and you're standing at the doorway looking out. You may be leaving for your own apartment, induction into the armed forces, a new career, college, or marriage. Even if you'll be staying at home for a while, you're standing at the door symbolically, because your hopes and ambitions are now turned away from the nest and toward life on your own.

Behind you are mud pies, childhood games, bruised knees, birthday parties, Little League strikeouts, family traditions, first kisses, B's in American Government, high-school proms, vacations with Dad and Mom, and Mrs. Jones's Sunday-school class. Behind, also, may be such traumatic events as a death in the family, illness, or Mom's and Dad's divorce.

Before you is the future, just out of sight over the horizon. You look toward it with a combination of hope, fear, ambition, excitement, and uncertainty. On one hand, the future seems bright and promising. There are worlds to conquer, and there are ambitions and gifts burning within you, seeking to be expressed. On the other hand, the future is threatening and uncertain. It threatens you with wars, disappointments, disease, accidents, and all kinds of hardships and difficulties, and you're not sure you can win in the dogfight known as society.

About three thousand years ago, other people stood at another doorway, looking out into a future which both excited and scared them. As the people of Israel stood at the threshold of the promised land, they looked backward to the good times and the bad. Behind them were the covenant promises of God. Behind them were the overseers' whips, the chariots of Egypt wallowing in the Red Sea, and the blowing sand of the hot desert. Behind them also were their grumblings and the golden calf.

Before the Israelites lay an unknown land. It was a land of milk and honey, a land of freedom from oppression, and a land of opportunity in which to establish homesteads and build a nation. But it was also a land of uncertainty and danger. It was inhabited by warlike tribes who lived in cities with high walls. How could a band of nomads, the alumni of the school of slavery, cope with that kind of future? They were eager yet afraid, enthusiastic yet hesitant.

To those people—standing, like you, at the

doorway of a new era of life—Moses proposed
a formula for facing the future:

> The secret things belong to the LORD our God;
> but the things that are revealed belong to us
> and to our children for ever, that we may do
> all the words of this law. [Deut. 29:29]

The Secret Things

The first part of the formula deals with the
uncertainties of the future. "The secret things,"
said Moses, "belong to the LORD our God."

The secret things are the things we don't know
about, the future that is hidden from us. We
don't know, for instance, how prosperous we
will be in June of next year, whether the family
circle will be complete, what the nation's economic situation will be, how Israel and the Arab
nations will be relating, if everything on the surface of the globe will be evaporated by a nuclear
reaction, or whether Christ will have come again.

God, in His mercy, has not allowed us to peek
around the corner into tomorrow. We have
enough things to worry about in the present,
without adding the things of the future. Tragedy
and hardship are difficult enough to cope with
when they happen, without adding the pain of
dread. As Jesus said, "Each day has enough
trouble of its own" (Matt. 6:34, NIV).

These secret things, said Moses, "belong to

God." God knows what the state of our health will be seven years from now, and He knows how proposed peace treaties will turn out. He knows about your family circle, and He knows when Christ will come again. While it is unfair to blame God for everything that will happen, it is fair to say that He knows about it in advance.

This first part of the formula has some implications for us. If these things are intentionally secret, then it is presumptuous for us to try to pry into them. It seems out of character for Christians to spend time and money on palm readers and fortunetellers, to scan the racks for magazines that promise "Startling New Predictions," or to search feverishly for the astrology column when the local newspaper is delivered. Neither does it make much sense to do with the Bible what the world does with the signs of the zodiac. If the future is God's secret, it is ludicrous for Christians to spend time counting the toes of Daniel's statue, adding up the numbers in the president's name, or adding the date of Artaxerxes' decree to sixty-nine sets of seven years, plus 119 days for leap years.

A second implication of the formula is that Christian young people need not spend time worrying about the future. It's in good hands. In the words of Jesus, "Therefore do not worry about tomorrow" (Matt. 6:34, NIV). Certain things in life are out of your control. There isn't anything you can do about them. "Who of you by worrying can add a single hour to his life?" (Matt. 6:27, NIV). We Christians are called upon not to waste nervous energy on things over which we have no power. Nor do we have to feel responsible for those things which are beyond our ability to change. We may simply leave them in the hands of God.

The Revealed Things

The second part of the formula is, "The things that are revealed belong to us and to our children for ever, that we may do all the words of this law."

We Christians are not to assume for ourselves the things that belong to God—but neither are we to leave for God those things that belong to us. While it is true that some things are in God's hands, it is just as true that other things have been placed in our hands.

There are some things that we have the ability to change, that we have authority over, that we have power to transform. God has given us brains, hands, and talents—and He expects us to use them. He has told us plainly in the Scriptures how He wants us to live, and He expects us to direct our lives accordingly. The phrase *Let go and let God* can, under some circumstances, be little more than an evasion of responsibility.

We don't know if we will be successful in our chosen career (secret things belong to God), but we know that we must work hard to achieve success (things that are revealed belong to us).

Likewise, we don't know whether we will graduate from college with honors, but we know that studying takes a lot of self-discipline.

We don't know whether we will die of cancer, but we do know the effects of smoking on our health.

We don't know how much rain will fall, but farmers know which seed, fertilizer, and cultivation are best.

We don't know how our children will turn out, but we know what our responsibilities are in rearing them.

We don't know what temptations we will face, but we have a duty to be strong as we contend with them.

We don't know whether a certain person will accept Christ, but we do know our responsibility to witness to people.

We don't know when the end of the age will come, but we do know that we must be prepared.

Does this mean that when we are dealing with the second part of the formula, we are completely on our own? No, it doesn't. As the Israelites moved forward, accepting the responsibilities God had laid on them, Moses said, "It is the LORD who goes before you; he will be with you, he will not fail you or forsake you; do not fear or be dismayed" (Deut. 31:8). Or as Paul said many years later, "Work out your own salvation with fear and trembling; for God is at work in you" (Phil. 2:12 — 13).

Thus we can move forward boldly into the unknown land of the future, grasping eagerly the responsibilities which are ours and leaving for God the uncertain tomorrow—for that belongs to Him.

Seeking God's Will— Commitment or Cop-out?

People today, including young people, are looking for something or somebody who will give them direction in life.

Dear Abby and Dear Ann Landers receive thousands of letters each week, and their advice columns appear in most newspapers across the nation. High school and college counseling offices are busy. Career testing and counseling is a growing industry. Horoscope books and magazines are hot items in bookstores.

Among Christians, this search for direction takes the form of seeking God's will for our lives. The revival of personal religion, known as the born-again movement, has sparked a new interest in seeking God's will. The National Sunday School Association polled three thousand teenagers from evangelical churches. The teens were asked to rate seven religious topics according to their interest in those topics. Ranking first was "accomplishing God's will for my life." The leading question of a popular system of personal evangelism is, "Do you know that God has a wonderful plan for your life?"

Christians are seeking authoritative answers to a multitude of questions: Whom should I marry, if, indeed, I should marry? When should we start a family? Should the wife work outside the home, especially when there are small children? At what point—if any—is divorce justified? When—if ever—is abortion a legitimate alternative to pregnancy? Should I attend college? If so, should it be a Christian college? Which one? What should I major in? What vocation should I enter?

In addition, a number of young people are going to God for answers to less sweeping questions. Should I attend a particular movie, play, or concert? Does God want me to buy a different car? If so, should it be a Chevy, Ford, or Mazda?

In seeking God's will, many people are using a number of special methods to find specific answers to their questions. Among these methods are the fleece test, the Bible pop-quiz method, and the special-sign method.

The *fleece test* is based on Gideon's experience with the dew and the fleece (Judg. 6:36–40). After it became clear to Gideon that he should lead his people against the Midianites, he tested for God's will by asking first that a fleece be wet and the ground be dry the next morning. When that happened he asked that the fleece be dry and the ground be wet. Many Christians are ap-

plying that technique in a modern setting, placing a fleece of some kind before God and asking Him to respond accordingly.

For example, two Christian young couples were trying to decide whether they should establish a Christian bookstore in their small community. According to the plan, they would pool their resources. The men would continue working at their jobs, and the women would quit theirs to devote full time to the store. The finances consisted of some inheritance money, some meager savings, and a sizable loan from the bank. Yet these couples felt strongly that God wanted to provide this Christian service to the community. They were in a dilemma between spiritual certainty and financial uncertainty. Finally they decided to put a fleece before God: "Let's apply for a loan, and if our application is approved we'll consider this to be a revelation that God wants us to open the bookstore."

A young minister, a friend of mine, put out a fleece when he couldn't decide whether to accept a call to another church. He had been notified by phone and by letter about the call, but he had not yet received the official document signed by the proper officers of the church. "If I receive the document by Wednesday afternoon," he said, "I will believe that God wants me to accept the call." The mail came Wednesday morning, and there was no document. He went to the post office just before closing time to inquire if a letter had come in. There was no document, and he declined the call.

The *Bible pop-quiz method* of seeking God's will involves finding a clue from the Bible. A girl just out of high school was deciding whether she should go with her parents to visit relatives or whether she should go on a sightseeing trip with a girl friend. After receiving a lot of pressure from both her parents and her friend, she concluded that God should help her decide. That evening her devotional booklet asked her to read about Naomi's decision to return to her kinfolk, and the girl decided that God was telling her to visit the relatives. When her friend objected, she said, "I must do the will of God."

A housewife, unable to decide whether to make a blueberry pie or a chocolate cake for her family, decided to search the Scriptures. She turned, by chance, to the creation story in Genesis and read that "God made to grow every tree that is pleasant to the sight and good for food" (Gen. 2:9). The conclusion was obvious to her: God wants me to make a blueberry pie. (I think she made the wrong decision. Blueberries grow on bushes, and cacao beans grow on trees.)

In using the *special-sign method* of determining God's will, the person looks for some amazing coincidence which indicates God's answer to his question. Leslie and Bernice Flynn, in *God's Will: You Can Know It*, tell about a woman who had received a travel brochure about a trip to the Holy Land aboard a 747 jet. She had the money and the freedom to take the trip, but wasn't sure it was God's will. She tossed and turned one night, then finally fell asleep. When she woke up she looked at her digital clock radio, and behold! It was 7:47 A.M. She called the travel agency to reserve her ticket.

These approaches to seeking the will of God seem to rise out of a genuine commitment, and they give evidence of a lot of faith. In fact, when we see our Christian friends so ardently seeking the divine will, we may feel like C-grade Christians in comparison. Nevertheless, something about these approaches makes me uneasy, and I'd like to raise a few questions.

First, can we assume that God is going to give an answer on our terms? Putting out the fleece means that we, not God, are deciding the rules of the game. We are giving God the choice of responding to the options we have predetermined. Is God obliged to answer? Is He not free to reveal His will in some entirely different way? I am haunted by Jesus' reply to Satan when he tried to make Jesus force God's hand at the pinnacle of the temple: "You shall not tempt the Lord your God" (Luke 4:12).

Second, can we assume that God is prepared to give us an answer now? Most situations of this nature involve a deadline—exercising an option to buy by next Friday, or answering an invitation by early next week. I find no guarantee

22

in Scripture that God will be the captive of my desk calendar or my appointment book. In fact, I read that "with the Lord one day is as a thousand years, and a thousand years as one day" (II Peter 3:8). In that case, my answer may come entirely too late!

Third, are these methods biblical? The student of the Bible is to be "a workman who has no need to be ashamed, rightly handling the word of truth" (II Tim. 2:15). To allow Naomi's decision following the death of her husband to determine the way I spend my vacation makes a travesty of Scripture. One would be even harder pressed to find a scriptural precedent for the decision to go to the Holy Land. The only method that comes close to being biblical is putting out the fleece, but this, too, raises serious questions. For one thing, Gideon put out the fleece not to find out God's will but to confirm what he already knew was his duty. Also, he asked for a clear-cut, undeniable miracle, not a happenstance; there could be little room for misinterpretation. And—most significantly—Gideon's method is not commended, commanded, or practiced anywhere else in all of Scripture. This incident was never again referred to by the prophets, the apostles, or Christ.

Fourth, isn't it possible that these methods can become a cop-out rather than a commitment? Isn't asking for a sign a means of shifting the responsibility from ourselves to God? If the decision proves to be an obvious bummer, one can always blame God for failing to deliver.

Fifth—and this is the most fundamental question—can we assume that God wants us to have a clear-cut answer from Him on every question that is before us? Does God have a preference concerning every decision we make? Is God's will like a puzzle which can be solved only by those who know the secret code? Does God have a blueprint in heaven for each of us—a blueprint which must be deciphered in detail before we can live successfully?

I believe that God has given us, as He gave Adam and Eve, dominion over the earth (Gen. 1:26). This is part of God's image in us. God has actually transferred some of His authority to us, and He doesn't expect us to come running back to Him every time we must decide between a blueberry pie and a chocolate cake. He does not expect us to view Him as a celestial Dear Abby, from whom we can expect specific answers to specific questions at specific times.

Whereas Judges 6:36–40 fails to give solid advice about finding God's will, one passage has clear and universal significance for the person who is sincerely seeking divine direction. That passage is Romans 12:2:

Do not be conformed to this world, but be transformed by the renewal of your mind, that you may prove what is the will of God, what is good and acceptable and perfect.

My wish for you, said Paul, is "that you may prove what is the will of God." According to commentator W. H. Griffith Thomas, "to prove" means "to know surely" or "to have trustworthy knowledge of." The New International Version translates this verse, "Then you will be able to test and approve what God's will is."

How can we "know surely" what God's will is? On the negative side, we are not to be "conformed to this world." That means that we are not to allow the world to "squeeze [us] into its own mold" (*Phillips*). It means that our values and standards are to come from some source other than the society around us.

On the positive side, we are to be "transformed." That means "to be changed, to be made different." It refers to the inward work of the Holy Spirit as He continues a process begun at the new birth. It is God's continuous work of re-creation.

This transformation takes place "by the renewal of your mind." That makes sense, since the mind is the seat of the decision-maker, the will. This is where the transformation process begins.

This, then, is the most important part of finding God's will—a renewed mind and a transformed inner self. Seeking God's will means adopting a new set of values, new criteria of what is important in life. The person who is thus transformed will have a new concern about such things as honesty, purity, justice, and equality.

When our lives and minds are transformed, *we will, in fact, already be doing the will of God.* God's will covers far more than the minutiae of our lives. His top priority is holiness. God is far more concerned about *motives* than He is about the decisions themselves. Whether you or I take a 747 to the Holy Land is relatively unimportant. What is important is the *reason* for doing so. That's also true of the decision about visiting relatives: God is far more concerned about our loving relationship with our kinfolk than He is about a haphazard discovery of an obscure verse in the Book of Ruth. The same is true about the opening of the Christian bookstore. The most important thing, in God's eyes, is the spiritual condition of the minds that made the decision. As it was, the bookstore failed and creditors lost thousands of dollars. However, if success were the criterion for judging whether people are following God's will, then the Pink Pussycat Adult Book Store and 25¢ Peep Show is dear to the heart of God!

While we are within the will of God—while we are transformed and renewed—we may make some faulty judgments and some bad decisions. And we will have to live with the consequences of our mistakes. But this does not mean that we have sinned, any more than a schoolchild has sinned when he or she adds two and two and gets five.

But, you ask, how can I make decisions if I can't rely on special revelations?

For one thing, we can use our heads. God has created us with minds, and He expects us to use them. He has given us the gift of common sense, and He expects us to use it. If we feel a deficiency here, James has some good advice: "If any of you lacks wisdom, let him ask God, who gives to all men generously and without reproaching, and it will be given him" (James 1:5). Note that we are advised to ask for wisdom, not for pat answers.

Second, let us take seriously the talents and abilities God has given us. "Having gifts that differ according to the grace given to us, let us use them" (Rom. 12:6). The nature of these gifts should be a prominent factor in our decisions. I, for one, never had to seek a special revelation from God about whether I should become a professional football player. He revealed that to me through my genes nearly a half-century ago!

Third, God has given us some very clear rules in His Word, and He has given us the responsibility of applying them in specific situations. Romans 12:3 says, "For by the grace given to me I bid every one among you not to think of himself more highly than he ought to think." Keep reading—to the end of the chapter, then to the end of the book—and you'll find more than enough information about the will of God. When I'm standing in front of a cigarette machine, I don't have to throw a fleece before God by saying, "If I don't have the correct change, I'll know it's against your will to buy a pack of Marlboros." Almost two thousand years ago God called my body a temple of the Holy Spirit (I Cor. 3:16), and it's up to me to put that principle into practice. In many cases, it's almost cynical to come back for specific instructions.

But what about those decisions in which there are no clear-cut spiritual or ethical issues? I venture to say that in such cases the good Lord approves of whichever choice we make. We are free to make decisions of this nature without fear of sinning. This is obviously true with such issues as blueberry pie versus chocolate cake (unless you feel a moral obligation to boycott one or the other on behalf of blueberry pickers or cacao-bean pickers), but it may be more widely true than we think. Take, for instance, my minister friend who couldn't decide about his call to serve another church. After considering carefully the nature of the two congregations, his own spiritual gifts, his family situation, and the condition of his own heart, he might have concluded that he could serve the Lord joyfully and acceptably in either place. I believe that a decision either way could be within the will of God.

God's guidance, then, does not consist of His specific advice on every decision in life. Nor does God play games with us by hiding clues in digital alarm clocks—or even in the Bible. Seeking

God's will is primarily living by Romans 12:2: "Do not be conformed to this world but be transformed by the renewal of your mind, that you may prove what is the will of God, what is good and acceptable and perfect."

That's a commitment, not a cop-out.

Daydreams

We all have daydreams.

During those boring lectures you've been picked as starting quarterback, won a leading role in a Broadway musical, or left on your honeymoon. On quiet Sunday afternoons in the park you've discovered a cure for cancer, were hired by the city's leading architectural firm, were awarded your doctorate in Arabic, opened your own hobby store, or gave a hundred thousand dollars to missions. While the stereo blared in your room you became a surgical nurse or successfully defended your welterweight title; your Hereford bull was judged best of the show, or your evangelistic sermon brought 450 people forward to make decisions for Christ.

Now comes the hard part.

Saying no to your roommate, who wants you to play racquetball instead of studying chemistry. Giving to God a tenth of your minimum-wage earnings from your part-time job. Doing calisthenics, even though they seem unnecessary and idiotic. Cleaning up your room and mowing the lawn. Practicing the scales over and over again. Going to church, despite the raised eyebrows of your dormitory mates. Getting up and going to work despite a bad case of the sniffles. Coping with tensions without losing control. Saying thanks, but no thanks, to a slightly-used term paper that's available for a minimum charge. Conjugating verbs, washing the dishes, making your paycheck stretch all the way to next Friday, and selling those twenty-five tickets (that benefit a charity) just because you promised you would. Working hard even when the boss is on a two-week cruise to the Bahamas, and accepting criticism with a smile.

There's a basic principle here. Much of life is a school—a school of small tasks. These small tasks prepare us for larger tasks, which in turn prepare us for still larger tasks. And we can't think seriously about the large tasks before we are willing to discipline ourselves to do the small ones.

Before we can run we must walk, and before we can walk we must crawl.

Before we fly solo we must fly with an instructor, and before we fly with an instructor we must "fly" in a trainer, and before we get into the trainer we must read books about flying.

Spelling lessons prepare us for writing sentences. Writing sentences prepares us for writing paragraphs. Writing paragraphs prepares us for

writing term papers. Writing term papers prepares us for writing everything from annual reports to books.

Ten-point quizzes prepare us for unit tests, and unit tests prepare us for semester exams. Semester exams prepare us for the tests of real life.

About twenty-five hundred years ago, God asked the prophet Jeremiah a question:

> If you have raced with men on foot
>> and they have worn you out,
>> how can you compete with horses?
> If you stumble in safe country,
>> how will you manage in the thickets
>> by the Jordan? [Jer. 12:5, NIV]

In other words: Jeremiah, while you are planning great accomplishments, how well are you completing small tasks? While you are projecting impressive victories, how are you handling present challenges? While you are daydreaming about passing the final exams, how are you doing on ten-point quizzes?

To today's graduate, the implications of that question to Jeremiah are still relevant. The race against horses and the struggle through the thickets will start soon enough. For now, concentrate on racing with people and walking on level ground. Your future depends on it.

One more thing. All of life is a school for the

life to come. In the parable of Jesus, the king says, "Well done, good and faithful servant; you have been faithful over a little, I will set you over much; enter into the joy of your master" (Matt. 25:23).

Parents Need Your Help Through These Difficult Years

To get straight to the point—you ought to be concerned about your parents.

They are trying to cope with a world radically different from the one they grew up in.

They are making decisions which will affect the rest of their lives.

Their bodies are undergoing changes they cannot completely understand.

Their children are moving out of the house, and soon they will be forced to relate directly to each other.

They are under a great deal of peer pressure.

And—very frankly—they have a lot of bad habits.

Since this is the case, you ought to do what you can to help. After all, your first responsibility is to those who are closest to you.

Trying to help parents takes a lot of tact; they tend to be independent and self-sufficient at that age. It also takes patience, because their habits have become deeply ingrained by nearly a half-century of practice.

Helping parents also takes love. Despite the fact that you may not always agree with what they are doing, you must never forget that they are still your parents. While you may at times be tempted to give up, keep in mind that they are human beings struggling for a sense of identity and worth.

Your Parents' Health

Let's begin with a few thoughts about your parents' physical well-being. The majority of parents are overweight. They eat too many sweets and they snack between meals. The situation will probably get worse, because when you children are all out of the house your parents will go out more often to restaurants. Ironically, they often eat only toast and coffee for breakfast, when nutritionists tell them they ought to begin the day with a healthful breakfast. Speaking of coffee, you ought to tell your parents that nine cups a day are just too many.

You should also encourage your parents to get more exercise. Chances are, they get into the car every time they go anywhere that's more than fifty feet away. Explain that when you borrow their car you are doing it for their own good, because it forces them to walk. Many parents spend all day standing or sitting at work; then they spend most of the evening watching television. Your dad probably bought a riding lawn

mower and then took up golfing to get the exercise he used to get by mowing the lawn. Then he rented a golf cart, so he joined the health spa to get the exercise he used to get while golfing. Encourage your parents to mow the lawn, walk on the golf course, do pushups, ride bicycles, and take walks.

The Dangers of Drug Abuse

You also ought to be alert for the telltale signs of drug abuse. Ashes in the automobile, bulging packs in the pocket, and a wheezing cough are indications that your father or mother—or both—are hooked on nicotine. Be alert, too, for the presence of Valium and other habit-forming drugs in the medicine cabinet. Your parents may not be aware of the addictive potential of alcohol, so this, too, should be part of your drug-awareness program. Remember that your parents are under tremendous social pressure from their friends, so try to be understanding while being open and firm about the dangers of drug use.

Your Parents' Friends

Since we mentioned friends, we ought to say a few words about them. Parents are the objects of a lot of peer pressure. They want to be part of the crowd. Therefore, the friends they choose are important. Unfortunately, parents often resent having their children choose their friends for them, and your criticism of their companions may bring a harsh rebuke. The fact remains that the couples they associate with often use coarse language, tell off-color stories, and stay out late at night. Sometimes the women make themselves look ridiculous by wearing teen-age fashions, and the men try to cover up their baldness by wearing wigs or combing their hair forward. They also tend to wear Bermuda shorts and T-shirts with wide stripes. Your parents may be the only couple on the block that hasn't had a divorce or an affair. This, combined with the changes in body chemistry already alluded to, can push parents into doing things their children never thought they would think of doing— or were even capable of doing. You will want to give them companionship and support as they face these social crises caused by pressures from both within and without.

Financial Pressure

Related to peer pressure is the financial pressure your parents are experiencing. Your Uncle Henry just bought a Mercedes; your neighbors across the street have a new Chris Craft which they display on the driveway; your Aunt Mildred just installed a huge electronic home organ (which nobody in the house can play), and your mother's old boyfriend is now the president of his own fastener factory. Your dad probably feels guilty because he can't afford to send you to Harvard, and his shoulders recently betrayed his inward pain when a young upstart was advanced to district manager. Your mother's self-esteem dropped thirty points when she decided to go back to work as a professional but had to settle for a job as a presser in a laundry. As your parents try to keep up with other parents, you may have to remind them of the value of the dollar ("Money doesn't grow on trees"), emphasize the need for economic restraint ("Is money burning a hole in your pocket?"), and point out that personal relationships are more important than keeping up with the Joneses.

Unacceptable Entertainment

You may also wish to monitor the entertainment your parents choose. That ought to be fairly easy, because usually they stay at home and watch television. When you consider that their TV diet consists mostly of situation comedies, game shows, jiggle programs, and cop-and-robber chases, it's no wonder that when you come home it's difficult to talk intelligently with your parents. Besides, they tend to slump in their chairs while watching the screen, and their posture deteriorates. Try to avoid a holier-than-thou attitude while correcting their television habits, however. Parents tend to become ill-natured when you talk to them about TV.

Beliefs and Values

Remember also that your parents are in the transitional years of value structures, social attitudes, and religious beliefs. They are running

headlong into a whole new collection of con-
cepts—abortion, homosexuality, living together,
racial equality, religious toleration, and pacifism.
Your generation has grown up with full expo-
sure to these issues, but your parents may be
struggling with them for the first time. (Remember, for instance, how angry your dad was when
you reprimanded him for using the word *nig-
ger*?) When they seem confused about the rapid
changes in the world, remember that when they
were young the word *sex* was probably not even
mentioned in the home, war was considered a
necessary evil, and colored folks were good as
long as they "knew their place." Your parents are
changing, but they relinquish the past reluc-
tantly, and often feel guilty about doing so.

In conclusion, I encourage you to be a positive influence on your parents during this difficult time in their lives. As much as you may
sometimes disagree with them, try to understand. They are at an awkward age. Life for them
is full of uncertainties. Some of their most dearly-
held beliefs are being questioned. It's a time of
transition and change. They need your love and
encouragement. With your help and prayers,
they'll make it.

The Parable of the Prodigal Father

(Adapted from Luke 15:11 – 32)

[11]There was a man who had two sons; [12]and the man said to his wife, "Give me the share of our property that is mine." And he divided the property between them. [13]Not many days later, the man gathered all that he had and took a journey into another part of the city, where he moved in with a woman he had met at a bar, and there he squandered his money in loose living. [14]And when he had spent everything, a great argument arose with his lover, and she would have nothing more to do with him, and she cast him out of the house. [15]So he began to drink heavily and lost his job, and went and joined himself to the bosses of the skid-row area of the city, who occasionally sent him into the manpower pool to do hourly work. [16]And he would gladly have eaten peanut-butter sandwiches, but he could not afford even that; and no one gave him anything. [17]But when he came to himself he said, "My two sons and my wife are at home while I perish here with the winos!

[18]I will arise and go to my family, and I will say to them, 'I have sinned against heaven and before you; [19]I am no longer worthy to be called your husband and father; treat me as a boarder.'" [20]And he arose and came to his family. But while he was yet at a distance, his wife and younger son saw him and had compassion, and ran and embraced him and kissed him. [21]And the man said to them, "I have sinned against heaven and before you; I am no longer worthy to be called your husband and father." [22]But the wife and son said to the neighbors, "Bring quickly the best clothing, and put it on him; and put money in his hand, and shoes on his feet; [23]and bring out the delmonico steaks and barbecue them, and let us eat and make merry; [24]for this our father and husband was dead, and is alive again; he was lost, and is found." And they began to make merry.

[25]Now his older son was at the shop; and as he came and drew near to the house he heard music and dancing. [26]And he called one of the neighbors and asked what this meant. [27]And he said to him, "Your father has come, and your mother and brother have placed steaks on the barbecue for the entire neighborhood, because they have received him safe and sound." [28]But he was angry and refused to go in. His brother came out and entreated him, [29]but he answered him, "Lo, these many years I have worked hard to support your mother and you, and you never

honored me with even a wiener roast, that I might have a party with my friends. [30]But when this father of yours came, who has devoured our living with whores, you have prepared for him a big celebration!" [31]And the younger brother said to him, "Brother, you are always with us, and we share together. [32]It was fitting to make merry and be glad, for this your father was dead, and is alive; he was lost, and is found."

So You Want to Be Great

You and I know who the great people are. They're the ones who make the most money, score the most points, move quickly up the corporate ladder, win elections, make the shrewdest business deals, and exceed the sales quotas. They're the people to whom other people say, "yes, sir" and "no, ma'am." They have the faces which are recognized in the crowd and have the signatures which can secure a loan.

In the church, too, there are the "greats." They win the most converts, tell the most dramatic conversion stories, sing the solos, write the best-selling religious books, build the largest television/college empires, are pastors of the largest churches, and are elected to the top posts in the synod.

You and I know—in theory at least—how to be great. We have to have ability and talent. We must study hard and work hard. We have to be resourceful, innovative, bold, and creative. We have to keep the old chin up and think big. We have to know the stock market, the retail market, and the real-estate market. Above all, we have to know the right people.

Two of Jesus' disciples, James and John, wanted to be great. They wanted, as one might say today, "a place of greater challenge in the kingdom." So they used the time-honored truth just alluded to ("It's not what you know, but who you know") and sent their mother to Jesus. Not unlike the Little League mother who pleads her son's inalienable right to a starting position at third base, Salome went to Jesus and asked that her sons be granted the number-one and number-two spots in the kingdom (Matt. 20:20–21).

Jesus didn't put Salome down for this. He gave her no lecture about the evils of nepotism. He didn't deplore James's and John's desire for a place of responsibility in the kingdom. Nor did He give them a lecture on the necessity of earning such a position by hard work and noteworthy achievement. Jesus did, however, make a startling statement about the nature of true greatness: "Whoever would be great among you must be your servant, and whoever would be first among you must be your slave" (vv. 26–27).

These disciples' ambition wasn't wrong, but their standard was. It's all right to seek greatness, said Jesus, but you must go about it in the right way. You'll achieve greatness not by receiving, but by giving. By God's standards, serving is more important than being served; honoring takes

precedence over being honored; stature is more important than status. What we are is more relevant than what we have, and what we give is more important than what we get.

In Jesus' topsy-turvy code of values, it's better to obey than to command. But then, what can you expect from someone who said the peacemakers will be called the children of God and the meek will inherit the earth (see Matt. 5:1–2)? The poor widow who gave but a few pennies, Jesus said, was the greatest giver (Luke 21:2–3). The half-breed and heretical Samaritan on the road between Jerusalem and Jericho turned out to be the unlikely hero of one of Jesus' stories, edging out such formidable ecclesiastical heavyweights as a priest and a Levite. On another occasion, when His disciples had been arguing about who was the greatest, He took a child on His knee and said, "Whoever humbles himself like this child, he is the greatest in the kingdom of heaven" (Matt. 18:4).

Not only did Jesus teach this theory about greatness, but He also practiced it. Would-be greats, He said, are to become servants, "even as the Son of man came not to be served but to serve, and to give his life as a ransom for many" (Matt. 20:28). He put His life where His mouth was. He practiced what He preached.

Keeping all this in mind, we can imagine that there may be some surprises on Honors Night at the Post-Graduate School of Celestial Christianity. Some obscure country pastors, for instance, may be judged greater than some ecclesiastical empire-builders. Some spectacled benchwarmers may turn out to be greater than some all-conference quarterbacks. Some plain-looking girls may really be greater than some gorgeous cheerleaders. Some meek and slightly off-key altos in the church choir may gain more distinction than those who are in much demand as soloists. Some haggard mothers may be judged greater than some heads of state. Some migrant workers may be considered greater than their landowners. Some bagboys may turn out to be greater than their managers.

It's not that God puts a premium on mediocrity, singles out underachievers for special honors, grants sainthood on the basis of poverty, or automatically gives prizes to nerds. It's just that the standard of greatness in God's kingdom is dramatically different from those standards commonly accepted by the world. On the final day, such criteria as bank accounts, conference records, credit ratings, stop watches, popularity polls, box-office receipts, sales records, and merit awards will be as obsolete as last year's hemlines.

Jesus' standard makes it possible for every person to achieve greatness, because the advantages of wealth, color, talent, and opportunity are irrelevant. God's standard makes it possible to achieve true contentment, for one is thereby freed from the tyranny of possessions and position. Jesus' standard is the great leveler, because it ignores the human distinctions of fame and fortune. God's standard of greatness is the only true one, because it cuts through the superficial layers of fluff down to the core of the soul, leaving the true self standing naked before God.

Famous Last Words, Overheard in a College Classroom

"As long as you study your class notes, you shouldn't have any trouble with the exam."

"Since I'm very busy doing research for my new book, I've asked a few graduate students to help me out occasionally with classes. I assure you that they will not be taking my place in the classroom for more than two or three sessions."

"I'm going to judge your paper only on the quality of your presentation, not on the position you take."

"There are nineteen copies of this book on reserve in the library, so you shouldn't have any trouble doing the required reading."

"I show no favoritism in my classes."

"I'm not going to intentionally destroy any of your cherished beliefs. I just want you to examine your preconceptions."

What Do You Do When Everything Nailed Down Is Coming Loose?

In Marc Connelly's play, *Green Pastures*, the angel Gabriel has completed a fact-finding tour of the earth and reports the results of his research to God. "Everything nailed down," he says, "is coming loose."

That's a fairly accurate description of our world today.

On the international scene, everything nailed down seems to be coming loose. Just a few years ago, Iran was a fuzzy puppy and China was a fire-breathing dragon crouched behind the Great Wall. Then, seemingly without warning, Iran became (to borrow the words of Jim Croce) meaner than a junkyard dog, and the Great Dragon began guzzling Coke. By the time you read this, a number of additional twists and turns of international politics will no doubt have taken place.

We thought America had a SALT II treaty with Russia about nailed down, and we believed the Old Bear was finally becoming a bit less aggressive. Then Russian troops invaded Afghanistan, and everything nailed down began to come loose—including the U.S. participation in the Moscow Olympics.

We rejoiced that for the first time in recent history the idea of war was unpopular, and we thought that the concept of an all-volunteer army was nailed down, but most young men now face the reality of registration for the draft.

There was a time when the great colonial powers—England, France, Portugal, and the Netherlands—had everything securely nailed down in Africa, Asia, and South America. Now almost every Third World nation on earth is at some stage of assuming responsibility for its own destiny, a process which alternately encourages us and frightens us.

On the national scene as well, everything nailed down seems to be coming loose. The bloody war in Indochina and the fiasco at Watergate pulled great spikes out of America's confidence in the integrity of its government. The graph that charts the inflation rate looks like the upward slope of Mount Everest. Gasoline is almost as expensive as milk. Young people are entering the job market at a time when ten-year employees are being laid off.

Everything seems to have come loose in the social structure. In 1955, everything seemed nicely in place. White people were solidly in control. Colored people "knew their place." Then came Rosa Parks, who refused to give up her seat in a bus in Montgomery, Alabama, and everything nailed down began to come loose. The Ku Klux Klan and many other flag-waving Americans ran around desperately trying to nail things down again. But neither cross-burnings, nor fire hoses, nor bombings, nor assassinations could put things back the way they once were.

While today's graduates were in grade school, most women still "knew their place"—in the home. And while those graduates were in junior high school, most homosexuals still "knew their place"—in the closet. But that has all changed, and everything nailed down is coming loose.

Everything nailed down seems to be coming loose in the family, too. The family structure of the Dick-and-Jane readers—Dad, Mom, and two or three children—seems to have been phased out with the Dick-and-Jane readers. According to an article in *Newsweek*,[1] there are currently twelve million children under the age of eighteen whose parents are divorced, and one million children a year suffer through the dissolution of their families. Albert Solnit, director of the Yale Child Study Center in New Haven, Connecticut, is quoted in that article as saying, "Divorce is one of the most serious and complex mental-health crises facing children of the '80s."

In religion, as well as in secular life, everything nailed down seems to be coming loose. Roman Catholics are singing congregational hymns, confessing their sins directly to God, eating sausage pizzas on Friday, and shamelessly reading a book which just 400 years ago was on the index of forbidden books—the Bible.

Baptist, Reformed, and Christian Reformed Christians are doing things which, a few years ago, only Lutherans, Methodists, and liberal Presbyterians did—going to movies, dancing, playing cards, going to the beach on Sunday, and ordaining women to church offices. Once-formal Episcopalians are speaking in tongues and raising their hands in church. Independent conservatives are cooperating with other conservatives in forming political lobbies.

Sometimes on a personal level everything nailed down seems to be coming loose. On Monday, everything seems to be going right. You have a boyfriend (or girl friend), a late-model Firebird, a summer job, and a place in the chemistry school of the state university. By Friday your boyfriend (or girl friend) has become "too busy" for a date, the transmission has gone out on the Firebird, you have received a two-week notice on your summer job, and the college has informed you that the chemistry building burned down.

The question is this: what is a young person to do in a world of change? How can you cope in an era in which everything nailed down is coming loose? And how can you help older people, such as parents and friends, live successfully in a world of such bewildering uncertainty?

I'd like to suggest two courses of action. The first may surprise you: we must go around changing things when it is our Christian duty to do so. When everything nailed down is coming loose, we ought to be the ones who are pulling out some of the nails.

Those who have been brought up in a conservative tradition may be inclined to believe that change—by definition—is evil. The beautiful old hymn, "Abide With Me," has these lines: "Change and decay in all around I see; O Thou who changest not, abide with me." For the author,

Henry Lyte, a good Victorian, change and decay were synonymous. Change, if not downright sinful, was at least highly improper.

But you can see by the examples already given that not all change is bad. Some changes have been positive. Others, although painful, have brought about good. The price of gasoline, for instance, has caused us to question our use of God-given resources, has reduced our dependence on foreign oil, has made us walk more, has reduced the amount of steel used to make cars, has helped revitalize our inner cities, has strengthened public transportation, and has saved tens of thousands of lives through reduced driving and reduced speed limits.

God's people have always been instruments of constructive change. The Old Testament prophets called for spiritual change, social change, economic change, and political change. They were disturbing people, because in an age when everything seemed to be comfortably nailed down, they went about pulling things apart. And they weren't always diplomatic about it. Amos, for instance, called the housewives of the chosen people "cows of Bashan" because of their languor and preoccupation with luxury. The king called Elijah the "troubler of Israel," but Elijah replied that the real troubler was the king, who was causing the conditions that had to be changed. The real agitator is often the person who wants to keep things just the way they are.

Jesus was an advocate of change. In the Sermon on the Mount, His teachings frequently followed the formula, "You have heard that it was said . . . but I tell you. . . ." He never contradicted the Old Testament, but He regularly contradicted the tradition of His people.

Jesus called for a change in the people's observance of the Sabbath. He called for a change in their attitude toward Samaritans, publicans, and Gentiles in general. He called for a change in moral emphasis, calling for love as well as for law. But most of all, He called for radical change within. "Unless one is born anew," He said, "he cannot see the kingdom of God" (John 3:3).

Jesus was opposed by the religious leaders of the day, who wanted things to stay just the way they had always been. Since Jesus wasn't content to let things be nailed down, they decided to nail *Him* down.

The apostles were advocates of change. Wherever they went, everything that had been nailed down started to come loose. At Thessalonica a crowd gathered around the house where Paul and his friends were staying. The mob shouted, "These men who have turned the world upside down have come here also" (Acts 17:6). When my family moved to a different city five years ago, no one gathered around our house, shouting, "LeRoy Koopman has turned the world upside down, and has come here also." That is not necessarily to my credit.

Down through the years, devout believers have been in the fight for righteous change. Often they've come late, and often they've been a minority, but they've been effective. The Protestant Reformation of the 1500s, the Roman Catholic Reformation of the 1900s, prison reform, rights for women, rights for minorities, education for all children, the rights of laborers—all were brought about by people who were not satisfied with things as they were.

The Christ who called us to be lights in this world and a leaven in our society challenges you (and even middle-agers like me) to go out and change things. Your standard is not to be your society, or your parents, or "the way it's always been done," but the Word of God. Do not be intimidated by those who in panic are trying to hammer back all the nails that are coming loose. You'll be in the company of the prophets, the apostles, and Jesus Himself if you take the claw end of the hammer and pull out some nails yourself.

Nail-pulling, of course, must be done with a great deal of wisdom and discretion. You are not obligated to pull out every nail you see. Not every custom is silly; not every traditional value is outmoded; not everything your parents have taught you is dumb; not every old standard of morality is to be smirked at; not everything old is by definition obsolete.

The first course of action, then, in living successfully in a world in which everything is coming loose, is to be part of that process in a constructive way.

The second course of action is to have a faith that will keep *you* nailed down in a changing world.

Jesus concluded His Sermon on the Mount with a story about two men who built houses on prime lakeside property (Matt. 7:24–29). One of them was in a great hurry to finish, so he built his house on the sand, laying only a superficial foundation.

The second was likewise eager to build his new house, but he took the time to dig down through the sand until he hit rock, and then he built the foundation upon that rock. He was up on the roof and sweating under the tropical sun long after his neighbor was sitting on the porch sipping a beer.

A few years later a storm came, and "the rain fell, and the floods came, and the winds blew and beat upon that house" (v. 25), and the house built upon a rock stood, but the house built upon the sand was destroyed.

In the springtime of life, young people are in the process of building. You are making some basic decisions about vocations, marriage, lifestyle, ethics, and God. An awesome chunk of your future depends on what you have already done and what you will be doing in the next few years. By the time you are twenty-one, you will have predetermined the direction of much of your life. There is much good weather ahead, we have reason to believe, but there are also storm clouds gathering. The way you build now will determine to a great extent how your life will hold up when everything nailed down starts coming loose.

The person who builds on the rock can be recognized by certain characteristics. Unlike the person who lives only on the surface of things, he or she probes deeply into the meaning of life. That person wants to know why he or she is here, what it all means, where he has come from, and where he is going. That individual is not content to just take one day at a time; he or she wants more direction than that. The one who digs to the rock below considers the needs of the soul as well as the needs of the body. That person will also begin, at an early age, to consider the meaning of death as well as the meaning of life. Any view of life which does not consider death is a superficial view of life.

It is possible to drift along, anxious and confused, through much of life, hoping for the best and not believing firmly in anything. But that kind of nonchalance ought not be confused with peace. Peace—true peace—can be based only on genuine security, and genuine security is possible only when a person is grounded on the realities that are timeless and enduring.

Further, the person who builds on the rock

is one who makes decisions on the basis of facts rather than feelings. The hard work of digging down to bedrock does not necessarily make one feel good. It feels better to sit on the porch and relax. The philosophy of the fellow who built on the sand is reflected in the bumper sticker which says, "If it feels good, do it." The individual who accepts that view of life makes all decisions accordingly, whether they be about work, school, or sex. And if the feeling is not naturally stimulating enough, the next logical step is to augment it with some kind of chemical. But the person who builds on the rock is one who builds a life on the basis of reality rather than on the shifting sands of illusion. He or she deals with the real world instead of an imaginary one. He or she believes in altering the topography instead of altering the mind.

In addition, the person who builds on the rock is one who builds a life on Jesus Christ. As Jesus Himself interpreted the parable: "Every one then who hears these words of mine and does them will be like a wise man who built his house upon the rock" (Matt. 7:24) and "every one who hears these words of mine and does not do them will be like a foolish man who built his house upon the sand" (v. 26). Christ calls on you to do more than give Him a place in your life. He requires that you make Him the foundation, the center, the rock, and the hope of your existence.

Even in the springtime there are storms, and

you may have already experienced some of them—storms of sickness, family breakup, or even death. But during the long hot days of summer the storms tend to increase. During your life the rain will fall and the winds will blow and the floods will come, and they will beat against your house, and everything that is nailed down will threaten to come loose. You will have economic problems, marital difficulties, employment problems, and health problems; how you cope with them will depend on how well you are building now. When everything nailed down threatens to come loose, you'll need a foundation.

At the end a storm will come which will rip everything loose—and I mean *everything*. The nails will come out of the sun and the moon and the stars and out of the universe itself, and each of us will stand before the God who created us. Then those who have dug deeply and have built their lives on Jesus Christ will be secure, and not even the rains and floods and hot winds of final judgment will shake them loose.

1. "Children of Divorce," *Newsweek*, February 11, 1980, pp. 58 – 63.

Playing Second Fiddle

Let's be honest. No matter how many of Dale Carnegie's courses we take, or Robert Schuller's sermons we listen to, or Norman Vincent Peale's books we read, most of us are going to spend the greater part of our lives playing second fiddle.

No matter how phenomenally we succeed, how high we rise in the company, how much wealth we accumulate, or how respected we become, somebody is going to be ahead of us. Regardless of how hard we try, we'll be surrounded by people who receive better grades, score more points, have more attractive bodies, make more money, sing more beautifully, raise more hogs, live in better neighborhoods, sell more wickets, or have a more exciting sex life. Most of us will spend more time than we care to admit saying yes to bosses, superintendents, foremen, district supervisors, presidents, inspectors, and chairpeople. And a good many of them will be—in our considered opinion—clods.

If this is indeed the situation—and I doubt that even Schuller et al. could deny it—then we had better learn at an early age to cope with it. Since we're going to be playing second fiddle for a good many years, we need to seriously consider how we're going to handle it. We'll be tempted, of course, to consider a number of negative alternatives.

One of these alternatives is to pack up our fiddles and go home. If we can't play first fiddle we can refuse to play any fiddle at all.

Most of us had a Stanley Egstrom III in the neighborhood when we were young. Remember him? He was the kid who, when he was losing or couldn't get his way, picked up his ball and bat (he always owned the ball and bat) and went home. There are a number of grown-up variations to that theme. "If I'm just going to sit on the bench, I'll quit the team." "Since I can't start out as assistant manager, I refuse to be a busboy." "If my motion at the committee meeting is defeated, I'll quit the committee." "If I'm not elected president of Alpha Zeta Chi, I'll join Delta Mu Pi."

Another possible reaction to second-fiddle-hood is to become critical of the other fiddlers—especially of the first fiddlers. There are plenty of other second fiddlers around who are more than willing to begin a whispering campaign or organize a griping group. "Do you really think she's a lesbian?" "They say he was transferred here as our manager because he got fired from his last job." "You know how she got that job!" "I'm not one to spread rumors, but. . . ."

A third reaction is to overact, to play second fiddle in such a manner that it attracts attention away from the first fiddler. Most of us have been bemused by the bit player in the high school junior class play who overplays his role when he gets center stage. The second fiddler may adopt a peculiar mannerism, dress in an outlandish style, or adopt a weird philosophy. He or she may ask shocking questions in sociology class or claim to be an atheist. You can bet on it—the young man whose car has the loud muffler and leaves a trail of rubber on the parking lot has little going for him except a reasonably strong right ankle.

All of these methods of playing second fiddle will probably result in either being demoted to third fiddle or being kicked out of the orchestra altogether. All three responses—as much as they may seem to be justified at the time—are self-destructive. Therefore we may wish to consider some graceful alternative approaches.

The second fiddler, for instance, may do well to acknowledge the fact that only a few can play first fiddle. Not everyone is qualified to be a leader. Even among equals, someone must have the responsibility of making the final decision.

There are times in life when it is simply necessary and right for us to take second place. That's the lesson some of us had to learn in childhood when a new baby made its noisy appearance in our home. Despite our suggestion that the intruder should be sent back to God, we had to accept the fact that never again would we be the only child. That process of stepping back and playing second fiddle will be repeated over and over again—when we enroll as a freshman in college, when we start a new job, when a son or a daughter marries, when we retire, and on a host of occasions in between.

Number one is a very confined number. There just isn't much room at the top. A company can have only one president, and a department can have only one head. Even world record-holders find that within a few years or even a few months they are back to playing second fiddle again. As Joe Louis once said, "Every man's got to figure to get beat sometime."

Another way to play second fiddle gracefully is to learn to recognize and appreciate greatness in others. Even though you think he's weird, you'll have to admit he's a genius. Even if she was just selected "Miss Rose Blossom" and you were third runner-up, you will do well to acknowledge that at least she does have nice teeth.

True, there are times when acknowledging another's good points becomes almost too difficult for the human psyche to bear—when Miss Rose Blossom, for instance, is the girl who stole your boyfriend, or when the guy who drives up to your house in his new Porsche is your brother-in-law. It's tough when the new guy in your sales department surpasses you in his third month on the job, and your kid sister—whom you got a job at McDonald's—gets a raise before you do.

It's easy to rationalize at times like that ("She must have paid off one of the judges with you-know-what" and "He's always been a brown-noser"), but such evasions result only in sour notes from your fiddle and quizzical glances from other people.

Third, we can play second fiddle gracefully if we recognize our own strong points and use them to the fullest. What's important is how well we play fiddle compared with how capable we are of playing the fiddle, not how well we play in comparison to the other fiddlers. Jesus' parable of the talents (Matt. 25:14 – 30) teaches us that we are to do the best with what we have.

Whatever we can do, then, let us do it well. That's all anyone—even God—can ask. And remember—the most dramatic gifts are not always the most important. (See "So You Want to Be Great.") For example, some people seem to be able to make money quickly. But there are other gifts which are far more enduring, endearing, and satisfying than the gift of making money. What's the value of being able to afford a new couch every year if you don't have somebody to sit on that couch with you?

The Bible contains a remarkable illustration of a second fiddler, a fellow named Andrew. All his life he fiddled in the shadow of his illustrous brother, Peter. Even the Bible refers to him as

"Simon Peter's brother" (John 1:40). For all we know, Andrew may have been tempted to quit the band of disciples and go back to fishing ("I'd rather be first in the boat than a nobody in the band"). He could have gathered the eight other disciples around him and started a criticism campaign against the boss's favorites—big-mouth Peter, temperamental James, and pretty-boy John. Andrew could have begun attracting attention to himself by preaching from a fish crate in the marketplace. But he did none of these things. He kept on being a loyal disciple, despite being the only one of the two pairs of fishermen brothers who was not in the inner circle.

Three seemingly unimportant incidents indicate Andrew's unique contribution. It was Andrew who told Peter, "We have found the Messiah" (John 1:41)—and Peter believed that unlikely claim. Later, when five thousand people were hungry in the wilderness, it was Andrew who brought to Jesus a small boy who had five barley loaves and two fish (John 6:8–9). Still later, when some Greeks said to Philip, "Sir, we wish to see Jesus" (John 12:21), Philip went to Andrew, and together they went to Jesus.

Andrew was the kind of person whom brothers believe, small boys have confidence in, and friends like to have around. Andrew's strong point was not leadership or bombast; it was plain old-fashioned friendship, a rare and beautiful commodity. He had an even temper, a deep sympathy for people as individuals, and the ability to bring out the best in others. He possessed the qualities of human kindness and quiet faith unknown to many first fiddlers. He was a second fiddler, but he played his instrument exquisitely.

That, in the simplest terms, is the fine art of playing second fiddle.

The Young Man
Who Had
Almost Everything

And a ruler asked him, "Good Teacher, what shall I do to inherit eternal life?" [Luke 18:18]

He was the sort of fellow whose name is on the list of "ten young men most likely to succeed."

He had a great deal of money, which automatically opened a lot of doors.

He had youth, which meant that most of life's opportunities were still ahead of him.

He had good morals. He had kept all the commandments from his youth up, a claim Jesus didn't dispute.

He had an inquiring mind. He came to Jesus, not arguing his point of view or voicing his grievances, but asking for advice.

But, with all he had, there were at least four things he didn't have.

He didn't have happiness. He found that there were some things in life that money can't buy— or even make a down payment on.

He didn't have peace of mind. For all his clean

living, he knew that things weren't right between himself and God.

He didn't have generosity. He was addicted to habit-forming possessions.

He didn't have eternal life. That was the greatest tragedy of all. He had all his eggs in one basket, and some day he would drop the basket.

Yes, he was a young man who had everything. Well, *almost* everything.

Whose Side
Are You Really On?

Billy Murdle was finally on our side. Every day after school we played baseball in the town park, and every day Billy Murdle and Jack Smiley managed somehow to get on the same team. The result was scores like 12-3 and 15-1, always in their favor. (Once it was 4-3, but only because somebody hit our only baseball into Mr. Westenhoff's yard in the first inning, and nobody dared to get it.)

Billy Murdle was on our side because he arrived late, and Jack Smiley's team already had an extra player. We eagerly counted on certain victory—the first one in months.

But a funny thing happened to Billy. Usually, if he got up to bat five times, he'd hit two doubles, a triple, and two home runs. In this game he hit a fly ball, two slow rollers to third base, a strikeout, and a blooper single to left field—at which time he stumbled over first base and was tagged out.

When we ran out to the field after that putout,

Bob Settlemeyer, our shortstop, said, "Billy, whose side are you really on?"

Billy didn't answer, of course. He just gave Bob a disgusted sneer. Billy walked home with Jack Smiley as he usually did, and you could see that they were still the best of friends.

"Whose side are you really on?" The answer we give to that question determines, to a great extent, how we are going to play the ball game.

The Bible resounds with that kind of question. God calls us to declare publicly which side we are on—and then to play the game of life as if we really mean it.

Beginning with our first parents, the alternatives are clearly spelled out: obedience or disobedience; life or death; loyalty or disloyalty. Take your choice. But you *must* choose.

> You may freely eat of every tree of the garden; but of the tree of knowledge of good and evil you shall not eat, for in the day that you eat of it you shall die. [God to Adam and Eve, Gen. 2:16—17]

> I have set before you life and death, blessing and curse; therefore choose life, that you and your descendants may live, loving the LORD your God, obeying his voice, and cleaving to him. [Moses to the people of Israel, Deut. 30:19—20]

> Choose this day whom you will serve, whether

the gods your fathers served in the region beyond the River, or the gods of the Amorites in
whose land you dwell; but as for me and my
house, we will serve the LORD. [Joshua to the
people of Israel, Josh. 24:15]

How long will you go limping with two different opinions? If the LORD is God, follow him;
but if Baal, then follow him. [Elijah at Mount
Carmel, I Kings 18:21]

No one can serve two masters; for either he will hate the one and love the other, or he will be devoted to the one and despise the other. You cannot serve God and mammon. [Jesus, Sermon on the Mount, Matt. 6:24]

No one who puts his hand to the plow and looks back is fit for the kingdom of God. [Jesus to a would-be follower, Luke 9:62]

So, because you are lukewarm, and neither cold nor hot, I will spew you out of my mouth. [the Holy Spirit to the churches, Rev. 3:16]

From Genesis to Revelation the challenge is the same: Choose your side! Be committed! Declare yourself! Take a stand!

Taking a stand is not an easy thing to do, of course.

For one thing, our society militates against commitment. These are days in which commitment is not the "in" thing.

Couples live together for varying periods of time, without commitment or contract. They want to feel they can choose different sides at any time without necessarily calling a halt to the ball game.

Many businesses seem to feel no obligation to honor contracts; many nations feel no obligation to honor treaties; many young people feel no obligation to support their country; many employees feel no commitment to their employers; and many students feel no loyalty to their schools.

Our support of a football team may depend entirely on its win-loss record. Our support of a civic organization may depend entirely on the way the president dresses.

Our society is fluid. We move quickly from job to job, community to community, friend to friend, church to church. Roots hardly have a chance to sprout new hairs before they are pulled out again and planted in new soil. All of which makes it difficult to know what side we're on—or, indeed, to even identify with any side.

Another reason for our difficulty in taking sides is that many of us have been disillusioned with the teams we were on. We declared ourselves and then were deceived. Some of us have been hurt by a church, a political party, a friend, a school administrator, or a boss. That leaves us disillusioned and confused. It leaves us hesitant to be bold again, hesitant to declare ourselves to be wholehearted supporters of any cause.

But we must not put God's cause in the same camp as man's cause; nor should we judge God's integrity by people's lack of it. "What if some were unfaithful? Does their faithlessness nullify the faithfulness of God? By no means! Let God be true though every man be false" (Rom. 3:3 — 4).

A third reason for our hesitancy to declare whose side we are on is that it's *easier* not to be committed. It's less of a challenge to be a thermometer than to be a thermostat. We're apt to be less conspicuous as chameleons than as butterflies. It's easier to float downstream than to swim upstream. It takes less heat to be luke-warm than to be hot.

Despite all the incentives to straddle, limp, vacillate, and hesitate, there are some compelling reasons for telling the world you are on Christ's team, and that you are playing to win. I'd like to suggest four.

Integrity compels us to declare ourselves. Jesus was right. No one can be loyal to two masters at the same time. It just isn't right to play in such a way that the opposite team wins. It doesn't make any sense to call Jesus "Lord" and then not do what He says. It isn't ethical to call oneself a Christian and then to undercut Christ's work. In national politics that's called treason.

Obedience compels us to declare ourselves. The Bible says, "If you confess with your lips that Jesus is Lord and believe in your heart that God raised him from the dead, you will be saved" (Rom. 10:9). To confess Jesus is Lord is to voluntarily place yourself under His lordship, His authority. It means being obedient to His will for your life.

Witness compels us to declare ourselves. Billy Murdle didn't fool any of us. We all knew which side he was really on. We can't fool anybody (at least not for very long) by trying to be on both sides at once. We Christians are called to be distinctive; to be different in a good way; to attract attention by the stand we make; to be hot even when everyone else is lukewarm.

Love compels us to declare ourselves. "For the love of Christ controls us" (II Cor. 5:14). Although one can give without loving, one cannot love without giving. God loved us so much that He gave. When we truly love Him in return, we also will give: of our lives, our commitment, our ambitions, our energy, our money, our time, and our talents.

When we do that, we will know, and God will know, and the world will know, whose side we are really on.

"Follow Me—Now!"

Another said, "I will follow you, Lord; but let me first say farewell to those at my home." Jesus said to him, "No one who puts his hand to the plow and looks back is fit for the kingdom of God." [Luke 9:61 — 62]

"I will follow you, Lord, but first let me see if my parents approve."

"I will follow you, Lord, but first let me go to a few more parties. As soon as I get that out of my system, I will settle down."

"I will follow you, Lord, but first let me get married. As soon as I establish a home, I will follow you."

"We will follow you, Lord, but first let us rear our children. They are so small now, and it is difficult to carry them along while following you."

"We will follow you, Lord, but first let us get our children through high school. We have to work six days a week to pay the bills, and the children are so busy with school activities that there just isn't time to follow you."

"I would like to follow you now, but I must first see if my husband will come too. I don't want to follow you alone."

"I will follow you, Lord, but first let me retire. Then I will have time to follow you."

"I would like to follow you, but it is too late now. I haven't done it all these years, and you can't teach an old dog new tricks."

Famous Humanists
Give Their Testimonies

In 1974, 120 philosophers, scientists, social scientists, and religious leaders met in New York and signed a document called Humanist Manifesto II.

In four thousand words the manifesto outlined a program for the salvation of mankind—a salvation to be experienced in this life only, and a salvation to be accomplished without any help from God. "No deity will save us; we must save ourselves," it said. Priding itself in being free of religious dogmatism, the document defends the right to birth control, abortion, divorce, sexual promiscuity, and euthanasia.

This manifesto is signed by such notable people as Isaac Asimov, author; Dr. Francis Crick, one of the discoverers of the structure of the DNA molecule; B. F. Skinner, Harvard psychologist; and Rabbi Mordecai M. Kaplan, founder of the Jewish Reconstructionist Movement.

Humanist Manifesto II reminds me of a question asked by a college student in a bull session:

"Why is it that when people get educated they become atheists?"

Someone in that bull session answered by pointing out that some of the world's greatest intellectuals are Christian believers, and that the premise of the question was incorrect.

Nevertheless, the question is a bothersome one. It *is* a fact that many famous, wealthy, and intelligent people are humanists, either dismissing God entirely or viewing Him as only a remote possibility. Was the psalmist right when he said, "The fool says in his heart, 'There is no God'" (Ps. 53:1)? Some of these famous and well-educated humanists seem far from foolish.

Without trying to answer the question ourselves, without entering into any theological arguments, without overtly defending our faith, let us give thoughtful consideration to what some of the world's most famous humanists have said about themselves and the success of their faith. We will make one requirement: we want to hear their testimonies, not in their young and brash years, but in their mature years, after they have had the opportunity to view their lives from a high peak and a broad perspective.

Mark Twain
(1835 – 1910)

Samuel Langhorne Clemens, better known by his pen name, attained worldwide fame as both

a writer and a lecturer. It was the opinion of Ernest Hemingway that modern American literature began with *Huckleberry Finn*. Children from seven to seventy continue to delight not only in the adventures of Tom and Huck, but also in the adventures of *A Connecticut Yankee in King Arthur's Court*, "The Celebrated Jumping Frog of Calavaras County," *The Prince and the Pauper*, and many more.

Mark Twain was a humanist.

In his autobiography Twain gave his testimony about life:

> A myriad of men are born; they labor and sweat and struggle for bread; they squabble and scold and fight; they scramble for little mean advantages over each other. Age creeps upon them and infirmities follow; shames and humiliations bring down their prides and their vanities. Those they love are taken from them, and the joy of life is turned to aching grief. The burden of pain, care, and misery grows heavier year by year. At length ambition is dead, pride is dead, vanity is dead; longing for release is in their place. It comes at last—the only unpoisoned gift earth ever had for them—and they vanish from a world where they were of no consequence; where they achieved nothing, where they were a mistake and a failure and a foolishness; where they left no sign that they have existed—a world that will lament them a day and forget them forever.[1]

The testimony of a humanist.

Bertrand Russell
(1872 – 1970)

Bertrand Russell came from one of England's most distinguished families, and he added considerable luster to the family reputation.

Russell first gained attention with *Principles*

---

1. Mark Twain, *The Autobiography of Mark Twain*, vol. 2 (New York: Harper Brothers, 1924), pp. 37 – 38.

of Mathematics (1903). Seven years later he published, with Alfred North Whitehead, a book which opened a new era in the study of the principles of mathematics and philosophy, *Principia Mathematica*. More than forty books followed, on such divergent subjects as philosophy, education, politics, and sex.

In 1950 Russell received the Nobel prize for literature and was described as a "defender of humanity and freedom of thought." He lectured at Cambridge, Harvard, the University of Peking, the University of Chicago, and the University of California (Los Angeles).

Late in life, in the early 1960s, Russell again came to the forefront of public notice by leading pacifist demonstrations against nuclear weapons.

Bertrand Russell was a humanist.

Like Mark Twain, Russell left a testimony about the meaning of life. In a letter to Goldsworthy Lowes Dickinson, he wrote:

> Why should you suppose I think it foolish to wish to see the people one is fond of? What else is there to make life tolerable? We stand on the shore of an ocean, crying to the night and the emptiness; sometimes a voice answers out of the darkness. But it is the voice of one drowning; and in a moment the silence returns.[2]

The testimony of a humanist.

2. Bertrand Russell, *The Autobiography of Bertrand Russell, 1872 – 1914* (Boston: Little, Brown and Company, 1967), p. 287.

Robert G. Ingersoll
(1833 – 1899)

Robert G. Ingersoll was a lawyer, politician, and writer. Most of all, he was an evangelist for atheism. With the possible exception of Madalyn Murray O'Hair, no popular lecturer has ever attacked Christianity so forcefully, widely, continuously, and effectively.

Robert Ingersoll's personal testimony is remarkably like that of Bertrand Russell. As Ingersoll stood at the grave of his brother and gave an oration, he said:

> Life is a narrow vale between the cold and barren peaks of two eternities. We strive in vain to look beyond the heights. We cry aloud and the only answer is the wailing echo of our cry.[3]

The testimony of a humanist.

W. Somerset Maugham
(1874 – 1965)

W. Somerset Maugham was one of the most popular British writers of this century. Best known for his semi-autobiographical novel, *Of Human Bondage*, he wrote a dozen novels and more than 150 short stories. Sometimes ignored by the critics, he was loved by the reading public. He died at the age of ninety-one, an immensely famous and wealthy man, but em-

3. Robert G. Ingersoll, *The Works of Robert G. Ingersoll*, ed. C. P. Farrell, vol. 12 (New York: Ingersoll Publishers, Inc., 1900), pp. 390 – 391.

bittered against his ex-wife and embroiled in a lawsuit with his daughter.

W. Somerset Maugham was a humanist. Near his life's end Maugham wrote:

When I look back on my life ... it seems to me strangely lacking in reality. ... It may be that my heart, having found rest nowhere, had some deep ancestral craving for God and immortality which my reason would have no truck with.[4]

The testimony of a humanist.

George Bernard Shaw
(1856 – 1950)

Those who have enjoyed the musical, *My Fair Lady*, have George Bernard Shaw to thank. His play, *Pygmalion* (1913), was the basis for that modern musical.

Pygmalion is just one of more than fifty plays written by Shaw. Some of his better-known works are *Saint Joan*, *The Devil's Disciple*, *Caesar and Cleopatra*, and *Androcles and the Lion*. He used drama as a vehicle for social reform, vying against slum landlords, war, and the oppression of women.

In 1925 George Bernard Shaw was awarded the Nobel prize for literature.

George Bernard Shaw was a humanist.

Shaw expressed his disillusionment through

---

4. Quoted by columnist Norman Ross, Chicago *Daily News*, January 26, 1964.

the mouth of the "father" in his play, *Too True to Be Good*, penned near the end of his life:

> The science I pinned my faith to is bankrupt.... Its counsels which should have established the millennium have led directly to European suicide.... For its sake I helped to destroy the faith of millions of worshipers in the temples of a thousand creeds. And now they look at me and behold the supreme tragedy of an atheist who has lost his faith.[5]

The testimony of a humanist.

Let us share just one more personal testimony. It was written by a man of immense intellect, great ambition, and genuine literary achievement; a man who also underwent great personal suffering and gross miscarriage of justice. Said he in his old age:

> For I am already on the point of being sacrificed; the time of my departure has come. I have fought the good fight, I have finished the race, I have kept the faith. Henceforth there is laid up for me the crown of righteousness, which the Lord, the righteous judge, will award to me on that Day, and not only to me but also to all who have loved his appearing. [II Tim. 4:6−8].

The testimony of a believer.

5. George Bernard Shaw, *Too True to Be Good, Village Wooing, and The Rocks: Three Plays by Bernard Shaw* (London: Constable and Company, 1934), p. 89.

The Outlandish Claim

And they all said, "Are you the Son of God, then?" And he said to them, "You say that I am." [Luke 22:70]

Sometimes what you think of a person isn't really that important to you. The girl at the checkout counter who overcharged you a dime—did she make a mistake or did she do it intentionally? As long as you get your dime back, you don't really care.

At other times your evaluation of another person is very important—the man you are dating, for instance. He claims he makes fifty thousand dollars a year as an undercover agent, but beyond that he is vague. If he is telling the truth, he may be quite an extraordinary fellow; if he's telling a lie, marrying him is likely to bring monumental problems.

So here stands Jesus before you, claiming to be the Son of God. If He is, you have found the unique person of the universe. If He isn't, He is just another nut.

If He is the Son of God, you had better dedicate your soul, your body, your mind, your life to Him; if He isn't, you would do well to have nothing more to do with Christ or the Christian religion.

If He is what He claims to be, you can accept all of His teachings and live wholeheartedly by them; if not, you'll have to write them off as a bad joke.

If He is the Son of God, the gospel record is a true and accurate account; if not, it is an elaborate and cruel hoax.

If He is the Son of God, He can be your Savior for all eternity; if He isn't, He is a self-deluded megalomaniac.

You can't suspend your judgment. The claim is too startling; the issues are too vital; the stakes are too high. You can't say, "Wait and see," because you'll pass this way only once.

The facts are in. The decision is yours.

You Become What You Think

Finally, brethren, whatever is true, whatever is honorable, whatever is just, whatever is pure, whatever is lovely, whatever is gracious, if there is any excellence, if there is anything worthy of praise, think about these things. [Phil. 4:8]

List of Sources

The following were adapted from previously published articles or books by the author:

"Famous Humanists Give Their Testimonies," from "Famous Atheists Give Their Testimonies," *The Church Herald*, July 12, 1974;

"Follow Me—Now!" from *Prayer Time*, December 21, 1969;

"A Formula for Facing the Future," from "A Formula for the New Year," *The Church Herald*, December 29, 1978;

"The Outlandish Claim," from "Believing in Jesus' Deity," chapter 19 in *Twenty-six Vital Issues* (Grand Rapids: Baker, 1978);

"A Prayer at the End of the School Year," from "A Litany for the Opening of School," *The Church Herald*, September 21, 1979;

"Whose Side Are You Really On?" from "Whose Side Are You Really On," *The Church Herald*, December 12, 1975;

"The Young Man Who Had Almost Everything," from *Prayer Time*, June 20, 1970.